Fractured Paths of Disheartened Minds

ISBN 10 - 0692359362
ISBN 13 - 978-0692359365

Printed in the United States of America.

10 9 8 7 6 5 4 3 2 1

Introduction

This book of poetry explores the realm of survival. Each poem reflects a point when a person makes a sacrifice in a situation... in many instances for love. It explores what happens when the person holds onto an idea so much that it consumes them. These notions conflict with their core beliefs and eventually forces them to become lost, confused, depraved, changed, and more. Through this conflict: a person adapts to the situation, kills to survive, or a part (or whole) of themself dies.

Eventually so much changes that the person behind the mirror is unrecognizable. Confronting issues of self image and personal value are brought out. After a while, it implores questions such as: How far are you willing to go? How deep have you sunken? Is it worth it? Should you shun it or learn from the experience?

Treat the book as an instrument to learn from defeating notions of self. The illustrations presented are symbolic portrayals of the poems. Life isn't always black or white. Most people travel through both colors mixing into shades of grey. To be blind is to see one side or another. To accept and grasp life there must balance. It is my intent to show a glimpse of paths that others have taken.

Inspiration

The books are my recipe for life.
Filling me with serenity and resistance.
This mission.
I checked.
Vexed by the occasion.
Slain to leave a stain on the land.
And demand profit or prominent change.

Sole I.

Medium

Fracturing spaces where others cannot.
That's how I'm able to frame sentiment.
The medium drags deep, within many moods.
It helps bring fruits from trees and tides from oceans.
It separates the commotion.
Choose to see what I want to see.
Placed in the middle, I live in reality or a split tragedy.
It's as if I'm winged, beaming onto fellow's esteem.
Propelling them to new heights.
Then I'm not, based like a shell or a rock.
Meant to divide delusion or cause fusion.
Did I mention I can burrow into the lot?
Turn the scenario into my plot.
A foundation to the name that I bare.
People don't care.
They don't even dare to be bright.
Or see the light in other's eyes.
They close the blinds against the breeze.
Not fulfilling their needs.
Honorable manners are too much.
But they still claim it.
Frame it into view.
Forsaken when nerves gets bent.
Too much spent on elaborate tricks.
When presented should I wear it or share it?
Should I fight or flight?
What if no one else sees the plight?
Can I break the surface?
Or will I walk all night?

Where's your home little one?

Where's your home little one?
Milling about for weeks.
So deeply immersed, the pressure normalized.
Much of what you remembered had splintered.
Fending for your own in a cruel world.

Where's your home little one?
In crowded streets filled with incumbent walls.
Dirty, tired, and weak.
Ruined beyond recognition.
Crying in a state of despair.
Why doesn't anyone stop to help you?

Where's your home little one?
Family long gone.
New kin forged along the road.
A purposeful blend of connections.
Who abandoned you to this fate?
Are you willing to share?
Is there a way to repair the damage?

Maniac

I can no longer ignore.
Determined to explore.
A treasure must be hidden.
If not then why am I driven?
What I'm willing to do to attain, hasn't been ordained.
And not likely at this pace.
There's a need to charge the race.
It's based on cause and effect.
Not neglect of the given moment.
I've wasted too much time.
Trying to calculate a rhyme.
These events weren't supposed to last.
But they've become the biggest blast.
Impels me understand my way.
Helps them feel at bay.
My reason is the beacon.
Far ahead of its season.
Unless you figure in the maniac within us.
Memories become hazy.
I would be sane and you would be crazy.

Cards

Play a game with me.
Dueling of the mind.
In time to define our standards.
My life is in your head.
Knowing you wouldn't be smart.
If in the end you can't beat me, then don't deny my right.
Waiting for the serenity of surrender.
Cards against humanity.

Flake

I'm a flake.
Sparked too eagerly with companions.
When it's time to manage, things run long.
As if seeking a way to lead me astray.
My comprehension is clear.
The hands of Father Time is clocking mine.
Not yours to decide.
Causation of a rift.
People react.
Regardless of what we've mentioned.
You can't guard intuition.
Once we do link, our composure is unique.
Completely absolved in the horizon.
So when you don't get a call or text.
Getting super vexed.
Just stick to the plan.
Know that I'll be your right-hand man in spirit.

Angry Man

Rest well little boy.
You've engaged the world with your friends.
Gave meaning to fleeting moments.
Grasped knowledge from the scene.
Yelling and fighting to be seen.
While aging into legitimate law.
All passed in the blink of an eye.

Calm down grown man.
You're strong enough now.
You were trampled.
Floating dangerously close to frantic.
But you continued.
Lived to breathe another day.
Bitterness is your only friend.

Speak easy old fellow.
No need to waste time bickering.
You're all you got.
Be prepared for the following day.
Brace your knees.
Shield your eyes.
Your mind will return to the sky.

Cold words no longer attack.
Whenever you want to strike back.
Throughout life we shun defeat.
Hoping it will never repeat.
To gain no foothold.
No strength to the cause.
Angriness is a huge flaw.

Box

What can be done to a box with a warped label?
Some mediocre tape and a shiny bow?
Reception of this may be granted.
The review will be slanted.
There are too many lessons for one to be jaded.
It brings me back to when hesitation existed.
Will the luxury be theirs?
Should they even receive it?
Do I really need it?
Can I truly achieve?
Will this make me feel supreme?
It wouldn't be measured forever.
Just wanted a pleasure or two.
A companion to shield through the storm.
Felt the need to be claimed.
So they sought to expose.
Steadily delineating from the goals.
It's as if they didn't share memories and expenses.
The treasure wasn't understood.
So it was rarely given.
The box I live in holds my dreams.
What if it's not enough?
How many charms can be stuffed?
Feeble attempts to comprehend the unseen present.

Dream Trip

I dreamed I was a guy who's missed his stop on the line.
Jolted by the sudden crush of reality.
People watch, appearing to be suspiciously elate.
Everyone hoping for my collapse.
My failure.
The trip and fall.
They say I'm one-way.
But I always come back.
In turn, I react to evacuate.
I bang and shout.
Screaming all about the land.
It's been taken.
No longer quaking to my moves.
I've fallen into someone else's groove.
Dry words and shallow actions are all that are given.
Hunting for hidden meanings in public places.

Prisoner

Not orange and black.
A prisoner clad in bright stripes.
Delightfully aware that I'm wanted.
My job makes me dance.
I laugh at their joy.
Can you rescue me from this monogamy?
The conundrum of repetition.
Its timeless dribble of onlookers.
Everyone clapping as I jump higher at their wishes.
Quicken my demise, I despise them.
Eyes get wide as pockets get fatter.
Giving me only a fraction of a slice.
A pie that we all crave.
Made to behave like cattle.
We're all about the matter.

Money.

Stay Locked

Do I hurt because I impulse?
Sparking masochistic desires within my blood.
Confused morals.
Wicked turns.
I rarely seek an answer.
Concepts becomes erratic when I start to measure.
My mind will bind too long with succession.
To be safe in the known, I fall to my own.
All I have left are four walls.
The locked doors and dusty corners are safe.
Poisoned, but controlled.
Protecting me from outsiders tearing to get in.
Wanting a show to put on.
Suited up and ready to go.
I stay here.

Fleeing Emotion

Those suspects I arrested, broke out today.
Fleeing from the Sheriff that I've risen to.
Locking away the glory of happiness.
Kicked back into the dark.
Smashing in the face.
It wasn't just the race or the style of the deck.
They neglected to pay homage.
Managed one role and sanctioned another.
My mental scope sickens me, as I inspect what has begun.

Hot Sleep

I don't want to wake up.
Not like this.
My vision was steamed.
Tensions were high in this field of fiends.
I tossed and turned as the fire stung.
A rhythm hummed of golden times and pickled rhymes.
It nurtured my nature.
My ashes burned and were churned.
Vessels swept to the side and back.
My mind relapsed.
The visions were re-awakening.
Pity in me grew.
Once I knew I had cast the wrong plot.

Appear calm, be rewarded.
Destined for circumstances.
Off to new beginnings made of fragmented endings.
Run through falling pieces of reality.
One will hit, crumbing further out of reach.
Aching for the life but not having will.
The struggle is real.

Battered Woman

I saw you twice last month on the bus.
Made such a fuss that many of us had to come clean.
Helped to restore your attitude.
On our first occasion you were torn.
Sworn you wouldn't do it again.
Ram daggerin'.
Bleeding internally from a ragged drunk.
Your claims hollowed out.
As your heart pumped cream.
Cursing his passionate sword.
Lust and lies paint your story.
Knew he wouldn't curb just at your door.

On our second occasion.
I ponder your current state.
It's no debate whether you didn't ask.
Your leg buckled with a splinter.
A little swollen in the face.
Didn't hesitate putting on make-up.
Shopping with a bit of cash.
Getting clothes to prove who you belong to.
"Good deals today huh?"
Your gapping grin showing the recess of several teeth.
... ...Not good enough deals.
Yet continuing to wheel through a line.
Lost her spine when ready to take action.

Turmoil.

The Shade

I see them smiling.
Anxious for my arrival.
But I feel a loathing.
Bent towards my destruction.
Speaking from afar, counting very close.
Burdening me with pounds that matter the most.
It's like I'm secretly hated.
Though it's not really covert.
Their smiles say, *"Hi."*
But their eyes say, *"Bye."*
"Why this skinny rat? Can't even match."
I don't ask why.
Don't even try anymore.
Many people aren't willing to explore self-hatred.
There isn't any love, when the rays shine in their eyes.
Just the shade thrown to shield me from their thighs.

Snared Adult

Regular strings don't work.
The needle and thread are missing.
Somehow I was trapped.
Straining to stay afloat.
Yearning for a place to call my own.
Heaven sends rainbows to everyone.
But mine was deflected.
Tell me what I'm supposed to do.
What about my voice?
It's choice in the manner.
Constructing has never been more critical.
Apart of the great law of mass.
Drain the power.
Crush the heart.
Adult-hood.
It's normal right?
Working becomes a joke.
Should I worry about the manager's voicemail?
Will justice find its place?
A reoccurring nightmare or structured tool?
It's all connected.

Scattered.

Out of Sight

Debt is your soul and darkness is your fortress.
Whenever you fail.
Look at where it got you.
No better kept.
No tears wept.
Just compelled to go further.
Why turn to me?
Must you gaze at the light?
Do you wish to snuff me out of sight too?
Is that part of the rite of being abhorred?

Her Case

Faster than a speeding bullet.
Kindness became her flaw.
She took the plunge.
Ignored the law of motion.
Making for different sanctuary.
She was mistreated.
Worse than anyone she ever knew.
The basket broken, far beyond repair.
Placing tender eggs should've been calculated.
Unsure of the battle.
Now she cries like everyone else.
When one realizes they're in too deep.
She fantasized gentle caresses and romantic dates.
Someone to show her quality love.
Not jealous fists casually thrown when in doubt.
Her struggle continued to grow.
A fortified companion was needed to battle.
One to fight away the storm.
New friends are in short supply and old flames die quick.
Docile bodies roam the land.
Will she pick from this heap?
Will she crawl to the next?
Cases are made for the numb.
Hardly ever are they dumb.

Fearless trekkers seek a thrill.
Never claiming responsibility for the kill.
Careful in the notion of insanity.
Chastise the foreign guest.
Soothing unless you touch it.
Hold on.
Close your eyes.
Poof.
Back in the air.
Dissemination.

My Wrinkles

Struggling to survive.
My nervous system shivers.
Erratically beating, I bet my life.
I did it.
It was all that was needed to do.
Forego lapses of judgment.
Loosen up the vines.
Gather into a bubble all that was dear.
And I did it.
I leapt out the side of your twisted logic and idol hands.
Now back in my mind, I will lock the doors.
Carry the weight of what's to come.
Stone washed and heavy soiled.
Lasted longer than the mental eye could see.
My wrinkles, a film that couldn't stain.
But would always remain, if I let it be.

Stride & Step.

27

Trapped Doors

All that exists is the moment.
Flashes ripped the scene.
Leaving gaps in places you weren't.
Can you give yourself?
Wholly nested in my girth.
Your essence shakes me.
Splits me into dimensions of seasoned steps.
I wonder which action was first to arrive.
Decisive.
You're calculated.
Testing mental prowess.
As I passed, you grew longer with each step taken.
Never forgetting the goal.
Further eliminating space.
Boosting from a tower, you stared at me.
Eyes glowing to match the night sky.
Each twinkle burning my choices.
Plotting my every move.
Craving the meat that protects my bones.
My skin paling deeper than the high moon.
Below my unnerved brain and nestling above my gut.
Shadows mark a path.
One done for certain.
You've performed this dance before.
Leading others through trapped doors.

Porous Shield

A hollow shield.
Minor protection.
From the fights around the corner.
Strained by the lights.
Many throbbing holes pumping.
Hard-core entertainment.
Bumping with space to fill.
The lazy one lasted longer than a season.
It became less dense and endued.
Rules to be obeyed.
But soon turned into disarray.
Mental decay re-arranged sight.
Just wanted the cream.
Didn't think about strife as holes appeared.
The tip percolating.
Looking for reasons to drill.
Too much energy spent sniffing after a sweet rush.
Not only does the sugar hold them up.
It saves them from the lacklustered realm of reality.
Traded so many desires that pores are sore to open.
Clogged arteries are mashed with candy.
Is it the creamy custard that made them come back?
Acting like the addict their mother used to be.
Could it be fought away?

Can't deal.
Had enough.
Truth comes knocking.
Push back.
Jump away.
Can barely stand to stay.

Holes.

Last Breath

She feverishly swims as she sleeps.
Trying to drown her body of fear falsely imprisoned.
She doesn't recognize where she's going.
Shell shocked from countless events.
Each labored breath making complications.
Her body is worn.
Untreated.
Sucked of flowing vitality.
Slumbered tears leak.
Vicious prophecies played over, forward, and back.
Repeating misfortune.
Belief in her heart taking its toll.
Closed the doors.
Shut her out.
Hidden in filth.
Facing the grim.
Double-crossed to depend.
It weighs down her soul.
Where few want to go.

Runaway

Never moving with the senses.
Fear is weaved into the grain.
Paying attention to the stark contrast.
The construction, a bold story.
Secrets made lies while the truth didn't weaken it.
Too sheltered to hurt cracked lenses.
What if everything is a lie?
Who can be counted on?
Muster up the strength to close the deal.
Basic mental capacity to navigate turf.
Regions of scarred skin.
Likely the threat of the red death.
Wobbling toward the pill box.
Little else matters.
Just a figment of the imagination.
It's always the case.
A sole cause of the break-down.
Mold the casket.

Hardly do I claim nourishment.
Though I am sustained.
I crave flesh.
Nothing less will suffice.

Junkie

I am a junkie.
Searching for a liberator.
Palpitate in the moment.
Needing to cancel the world.
When waves of oppression begin to lap at me,
My sins become the fins that push me through.
The inner space is transfixed using piercing moans.
The darkness submerges as words aren't spoken.
It's from pain I felt when judgment set in.
From high in the clouds, perched on faith.
Placed out of reach without ever knowing why.
Hands in their pocket and a grin on their face.
Ruined my world when they decided to lace my desires.
Blotched despair greets reality.
Sedation brings that elevation.
Motivated by the next high.
Frightening in its initial hurling.
Freefalling from the sky.
As bone becomes dust, peace comes to life.
Pop a pill.

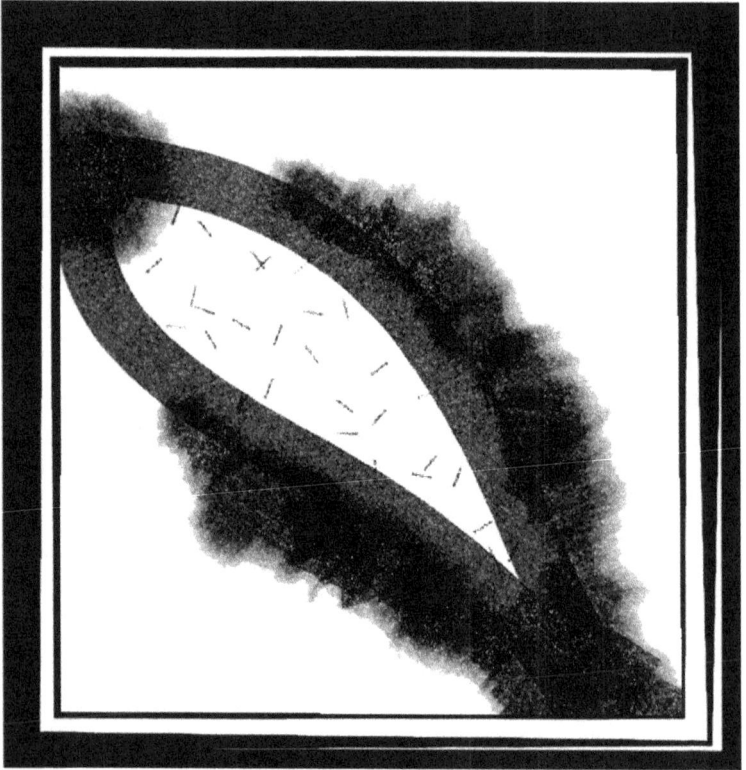

Loaded.

Outcast

The only savior is the virus that leaches off me.
Seeping through spaces like never before.
Mending my existence.
Providing safe release.
The lengthening arcs have sharpened.
Chiseling us away from them.
Another speck of dust clogging my eye.
Weighed down with viral suppression.
Its deception becomes my truth.
I embrace the arc and its unforeseen shadows.
As I give, it breathes days of sanguinity.
Realizing where the power is.
A consequence of its command.
Its sanctity.
The peace that keeps it whole.
Unforgiving in nature.
Baited with sedatives.
Reacting to unguided forces.
My torment perished when the nourishment began.

Wish

If I had a wish, would I still be here?
The world could be better.
I wouldn't have to share suffering.
Fair to all.
Damaging to none.
Except those who seek.
People could appreciate pain instead of propagating it.
Perceptions would be clearer.
Lack of space wouldn't exist.
I wish family meant everyone.
Commitment came automatically with someone.
I wouldn't have to constantly have to hide my fright.
Or bargain when little is left in sight.
I drift towards incidents that matter most.
Those who are supposed to be kin.
We could begin again.
This host of delusions exemplifies my mental exclusion.
When I decide the time is nigh or grave.
Can I live in this world?
Trapped on tap.
Ready to collapse.

Hate Through Love

She attained her partner's prayers.
Seeking refuge in the dreams.
As they came true, she knew little else to do.
Boredom set-in and anguish soared.
All the things she loved was deplorable.
The dream became a nightmare.
The heart just wanted to rush.
Relationships always seemed to put her in a rut.
Discovering hate through love.

Phantom Slave

No one has a clue of the repercussion that's due.
The world has turned.
One bridge burned.
The third will break.
Scraping the edge of how much one can take.
Until breaking into the flesh, hurting a little less.
Each personal demon becoming a stricter lesson.
By flogging my glee, I'm scarred like the devils past.
You made the choice and displayed me.
I was praised in your honor.
Little was known of the sacrifice.
I was a trophy in your narcissistic order.
That's the blueprint we're stuck with.
The damage was best once you accessed my inner self.
Mold my future as you see fit.
Meek, chic, and miserably bleak.
When you're around, comforting hallucinations are found.
It's your halo that flashes brightest.
Darkest when the rays fall.
Which of those do you obey?
Can you abolish a law?
To slay my name and slash my skin.
You need to control me.
An essence is known to those who see.
You only see when I'm gone.
Left in the dust, to rise at dusk.
Have you missed me while defeated?
Will you grin as I fall?
You'll be my reason to suffer, every lash of the law.
Pull the air from my lungs.
Milk the strength from my limbs.
You're the apple of my eye.
The fruit of my grave.
Enacted to be your phantom slave.

Bound.

41

Sticks & Stones

I am stoned.
I know my place in the system.
Not to develop.
Left to plunder.
Three strikes you're out.
Almost guaranteed to be hit twice by the gun.
Tell you who you can be.
What you will see.
Where you can't live.
Except in a room.
Encroached with revolving bills.
Stress becomes the test.
I rock in place, knowing this was the scheme.
I'd wait to say goodbye.
Thoughts verging vengefully close.
Tearing my flesh.
I was shunned.
No longer a function of the equation.
Just a page filled with unreadable scribble.
My bruised ribs hurt from the last attack.
Knocked out cold.
Confusion shattered as I spin to the ground.
The veto occurred.
My blood gone.
Execution was essential.
I was pierced with sticks.

If it was me.
I wouldn't propel myself into a system.
A flux.
Those who tell you what to do.
Who to screw.
How to behave.
I wouldn't be a slave.
Made craven by emotion.

Wrong Team

The poor or bold get told, "Never Surrender Your Dreams."
They don't notice when it's taken.
Told to jump and seldom for the right team.
Near doom is genuine fortune, while cashing from the sky.
Fixed being higher than thou.
Change the game.
Still locked in.
When you bend the knee, roots are damaged.
Too bad the mailman already came.
No checks in hand.
Just one extra bill.
Contracted through necessity.
Constantly battling for space to exist.
Fought over people trusted and mostly true.
Relief is in the belief shared:
Unthinking, not caring, or dumping the lightest hunch.
Polished stone shows effort in a semi-glamorous being.
Or show the extent of another's self-meaning.
People deem worthy either way.
Forced to hold yourself and boast.
Smile and be polite.
Hope that the day goes smooth.
Up the creek, the fountain should spray.
Tons of players try to cross the bay.
Stuck without a paddle.
Unwilling to accept the feat or find another display.
Hide and defy an abysmal day.

Failed Attempt

The symphony faded.
Stillness rocks the plates.
A short release into the atmosphere.
This will not be what you want to hear.
Your expressions have become my depression.
Commemoration will not be solely decided.
Proctors are needed to deliberate.
My biasness has me spent.
Fortunate shadows take precise caution.
The sleep isn't thick and data won't sync.
Siphoned into the night void.
Out from the light.
An angel ceases to cry.
The lullaby only kept me awake.
It's my imagination, primed and intact.
I foster these images.
The pain is a mother.
All of this sadness.

The Guide

The guide is a voice.
Bringing annulled resolution.
Unsure of the location.
Waiting for arrival.
Through the eyes of the beholder.
Lead to their path of envisioned sums.
Using righteous terms to execute a proclamation.
Based on the words of the other.

He quivers when he thinks about the one he loves.
Never being held to the proper degree.
Slanted towards the busted heart of husbandry.
Until he decided to mumble hoarsely.
Inundated by aggravation.
His methods are tumbled over.
Devising a fate, he found safety.
Irate and unsure of who to blame.
They grew apart after too many spats.
Their silence.
His comfort.
Her power.
To influence the way she wants.
So they abuse each other.
The less he says.
The stronger she grows.
He deflates his ego.
She spits fire.
Trapped in the cage of rage.
With nowhere to flee, life slowly churns to a cinder.

Mistrusting deeds can quickly be forgiven.
Many will choose to live in thoughts from the past.
That will be an issue.
It's clear.
Their guide is lost.

Headache

The beating inside my head.
Pulsating with each ring.
It stings.
Solitary turmoil is fine.
But dining on the feces of another's illusion is torture.
Conversation gets old relatively quick.
The confusion that's caused, should make everyone pause.
But many strain for tighter constraint.
So they bulge, not ready to take the fall.
Remaining motionless with flaws for all who seek humility.
This patron doesn't pay.
They just beg for service.
Exhumed from a tragic history.
Releasing their remaining humanity.
The streets are no longer safe.
Trenches feel like an eternal space.
Devoid of special notices with liberal causes.
Expecting to find a way to end it.
Wrong.
Just the throb.
Long, slow, and agonizing.

Ghosts

The death of self.
A birth of us.
A new us that wasn't desperate for the conventional.
You believed because you didn't see what happened.
Your faith waivered.
Encapsulated in the glory of the way.
Regret your past.
Forget melting today.
Savor the future.
It will be the only way to last the aching.

It stems from a living body we once shared.
No longer able to repair damage taken.
I was open to becoming Casper.
Helped the world to know a truer sense of you.
Envelope sanctity in your rendition.
A tradition that became another mission uncompleted.
While depleted, we attempted a different score.
Forced to stop the preservation of loneliness.
One unexplored with a destiny of alternate landscapes.
Where co-existence slept on an imaginary mountain.
The turmoil scattered in clouds of smoke.
We dashed towards the cliff and tripped.
I wondered with fright at Frankenstein's delight.
It showed how much you knew.

Noticing such, I rushed a new ending.
To escape our fractured beginnings.
Events that we kept reliving.
Our friction harbors transient memories.
I cherish these but they are too difficult to manage.
The monster itself was slain.
I began to shovel.
To gain no appreciation.

The past was buried at the funeral.
Leaving me vulnerable to new submissions.
Wanting useless information to calm maimed nerves.
To seek a resolute plan.
Was it all real?
It's past a blur.
There is an existence in between us.
When you mingle with ghosts, many people become clear.

All Over.

Bleed Like Me

Now all I do is bleed.
Waiting to hear from an unmarked call.
Letting you know that I stabilized from a fall.
It shouldn't have happened at all.
There are parts that can't be undone.
When the heart isn't one.
Congruity is missing.
Not the thought, the action each second.
Mismatching is the answer.
The matter that sums my host.
Across the coast of the terrain.
I've grown afraid of these choices.
Thinking a lush like me could be redeemed.
We are just a bunch of ravens.
Bringing demise throughout the sky.
Draping the world in overcast.
The needle dips into the ink.
I've bleed too much.

I'm feeling lifted on a slope.
Not willing to cope with sensations.
These qualms give me sweaty palms.
It's another nail in the lid.
Go up in the shadows, out of the mind's eye.
Can't hold too much more bottled madness.

Open Core

I rest with my wounds open wide.
Never before had a pain felt greater.
Paralyzing to the core.
The warming throb of universal loss.
Candle's liquid still is burning.
Seeping in my skin.
Coursing through my veins.
I cross sights into a mine.
Littered with the breaking dawn.
Mysterious feet step on my fingers.
Letting go of the world.
Wonder if the sheep ever sleep.
Waking up in heaven.
I haven't seen.
I've only felt.
Through the loss.
The utter loss of consciousness.

I invoke thee.

To be able to assess what is multifaceted.
Head to the unknown, so that I may roam in silence.
Surrendered my might.
Gaining an upper hand in the major fight.
This spirit is elusive yet cohesive to those who can divine.
Its existence summoned in words.
Engraved in the skin of history.
The wounds reflect the tenderness of the trust.
I still thrust into a new occasion.
Shake emotional figments from the mind.
Hopefully with time the magic will bind with devotion.
Receiving the message is not always powerful.
Every little bit helps.
Could be uttered with a single word.
The feeling within must be felt not just heard.
I summon this spirit, when it's time to do the bid.
Help rid myself of delusion.
Choose the middle, not scattered along a grid.
Everything isn't just black and white.
This path is pivotal to see.
I'll seek it out later to prove the potency.

I release thee.

Eternal.

About The Author

Carlton Rolle has had the opportunity to observe and live in various lifestyles. These places influenced the core of what made up his value system. Throughout all of the experiences, he began to understand that everyone has a story to tell regardless of their socio - economic, religious, racial, sexual, historically-based beliefs, etc.

Carlton graduated from Michigan State University with a Bachelor's degree in Liberal Arts. He then attained a Master's degree in Business Administration from University of Phoenix. With life experiences and knowledge from academia to support himself, Carlton began working for several magazines and blogs. During this time he explored writing in creative genres.

In Carlton's life, language acts as another mode of visionary expression. Writing sets the stage for thoughts and knowledge to be shared. He believes that people who connect with others have greater understanding of themselves. Carlton wants to enrich the world with artistic forms of expression from the mind, body, and soul of an experience.

To Stay Updated Visit:
www.soadioh.com

www.ingramcontent.com/pod-product-compliance
Lightning Source LLC
Chambersburg PA
CBHW071734020426
42331CB00008B/2020